# Balkenhol

## Dichte und Licht

## INHALT / CONTENTS

| | |
|---|---|
| 07 | Zum Geleit / Introduction |
| 09 | Lyrische Abstraktion / Lyrical Abstraction |
| 23 | Landschaft / Landscape |
| 51 | Akt und Figur / Nudes and Figures |
| 95 | Ecce Homo / Ecce Homo |
| 147 | Portrait / Portraits |
| 161 | Stillleben / Still Life |
| 189 | Vita / Biography |
| 190 | Ausstellungen / Exhibitions |
| 191 | Dank / Acknowledgements |
| 192 | Impressum / Impressum |

# INTRODUCTION

The present monograph, "Ballehr: Density and Light", is the first to provide a general survey of the many facets of the oeuvre of the Munich painter and draughtsman Ballehr. Before this the only record has been a folder of reproductions from the series "ECCE HOMO", although Ballehr's works have been for many years one of the highlights of the regional art scene.

Even when he was still young, Ballehr's artistry was moulded by impressions from the masterly drawings of Leonardo da Vinci, Hokusai's delicate woodcuts and Willem Kalf's luminous still lifes. These were the formative experiences which led to his spontaneity and surety in drawing, his art of omission in favour of the delicate line, and his concentration on the phenomena of light.

The monograph largely follows the development of his work. It begins with the Lyrical Abstraction of the 70s and 80s and leads via the Figure Groups of the 90s to the "Light Paintings" of around 2000.

Ballehr, incidentally, likes to quote Hokusai, who said, "When I reach 90 I shall penetrate to the inwardness of all things, and at 100 I shall certainly attain to an indescribable higher perfection. But only when I reach 110 will everything, every dot and every line, signify life itself."

Dr Gabriele Holthius
Museum und Galerie im Prediger,
Schwäbisch Gmünd

## ZUM GELEIT

Die vorliegende Monographie „BALLEHR: DICHTE UND LICHT" vermittelt erstmals einen Überblick über das vielfältige Werk des Münchener Malers und Graphikers Ballehr. Bisher lag nur eine Mappe mit Abbildungen aus der Serie „ECCE HOMO" vor.
Dabei gehören Ballehrs Werke seit vielen Jahren zu den Highlights der regionalen Kunst-Szene.

Ballehr empfing schon in früher Jugend prägende Eindrücke durch Leonardo da Vincis meisterhafte Zeichnungen, Hokusais sensible Holzschnitte und Willem Kalfs lichtdurchflutete Stillleben.
Aus diesen Prägungen resultieren Ballehrs Spontanität und Sicherheit in der Zeichnung, seine Kunst des Weglassens zugunsten der feingliedrigen Linie und seine Konzentration auf die Erscheinungen des Lichts.
Die Monographie folgt weitgehend der Entwicklungslinie des Werks: Sie beginnt mit der Lyrischen Abstraktion der 70-er und 80-er Jahre und führt über die Figurengruppen der 90-er Jahre zu den „Licht-Bildern" der Jahre um 2000.

Übrigens beruft sich Ballehr gerne auf Hokusai, der sagte:
„Mit 90 Jahren werde ich in das innerste Wesen aller Dinge eindringen und mit 100 sicherlich zu einer höheren, unbeschreiblichen Vollkommenheit aufsteigen. Werde ich aber erst 110 Jahre erreicht haben, so wird alles, jeder Punkt und jede Linie das Leben selbst bedeuten".

Dr. Gabriele Holthius
Museum und Galerie im Prediger,
Schwäbisch Gmünd

## LYRICAL ABSTRACTION

When I was at art college and in the subsequent
years my art was non-representative.
I studied the principles of form, such as the
expressiveness of colour, the way in which
surface contrasts determine form,
and the quality of lines, for instance that of
positive and negative diagonals.
These compositional studies of mine led to a
Lyrical Abstraction  -  perhaps comparable with
music.
Thereupon Professor Rudolf Yelin conceived,
for my exhibition on receiving my first degree,
the title which is still valid today,

        "Density and Light"

                      Ballehr

## LYRISCHE ABSTRAKTION

Während meines Studiums und in den folgenden
Jahren malte ich gegenstandslos.
Ich studierte gestalterische Grundlagen,
wie die Ausdruckswerte der Farbe,
die Kraft der Flächenkontraste
und die Qualität der Linien, wie z.B. die der
positiven und der negativen Diagonale.
Diese Kompositionsstudien führten bei mir
zu einer - vielleicht der Musik vergleichbaren -
Lyrischen Abstraktion.
Folgerichtig fand Professor Rudolf Yelin für meine
Examensausstellung den Titel, der bis heute
gültig blieb:

„Dichte und Licht".

Ballehr

SEITE 10/11: NOCTURNO
Öl auf Leinwand / Oil on canvas 94 x 130 cm 1968

GENESIS:

FÜLLE DES LICHTS / FULLNESS OF LIGHT
Öl auf Leinwand / Oil on canvas 200 x 200 cm 1999

GENESIS:

SCHÖPFUNG DER PFLANZEN /
CREATION OF PLANTS

Öl auf Leinwand /
Oil on canvas
200 x 200 cm  1999

GENESIS:

SCHEIDUNG DER WASSER /
DIVISION OF THE WATERS

Acryl und Öl auf Leinwand /
Acrylic and oil on canvas
200 x 200 cm     1999

GENESIS:

DIES IRAE

Acryl und Öl auf Leinwand /
Acrylic and oil on canvas
200 x 200 cm        1998

GENESIS: Ausstellung Johanniskirche / Exhibition St John's Church, Schwäbisch Gmünd, 1999

## LANDSCAPE

In fact I do not paint landscapes. Apart from a very few instances, such as the "Höri" on Lake Constance (1980), I have produced no "outdoor" paintings.
My landscapes are "free light spaces". They are developed entirely from colour.
Warm/cool contrasts and colour perspectives evoke the impression of light, air and depth; create atmospheres.

                                                                   Ballehr

## LANDSCHAFT

Landschaften male ich eigentlich nicht.
Bis auf wenige Bilder, wie z.B. die von der Höri am
Bodensee (1980) habe ich keine „plein-air-Malerei"
gemacht.
Meine Landschaften stellen „Frei-Licht-Räume" dar.
Sie sind ganz aus der Farbe heraus entwickelt.
Warm-Kalt-Kontraste und Farbperspektive
erwecken den Eindruck von Licht, Luft und Tiefe,
schaffen Stimmungsbilder.

            Ballehr

PAPPELN IN HÖRI / POPLARS IN HÖRI
Öl auf Leinwand / Oil on canvas  52 x 75 cm  1978

FJORD

Acryl und Öl auf Leinwand /
Acrylic and oil on canvas
140 x 160 cm  1980

Seite 28/29
ABZIEHENDES GEWITTER / PASSING STORM
Öl auf Leinwand / Oil on canvas   80 x 100 cm   1979

ISLAND / ICELAND
Öl auf Leinwand / Oil on canvas   98 x 78 cm   1989

FJELL
Öl auf Leinwand / Oil on canvas  80 x 60 cm  1996

STUIFEN
Öl auf Leinwand / Oil on canvas  50 x 35 cm  1974

KYZYL KUM
Öl auf Leinwand / Oil on canvas  80 x 100 cm  2010

SEITE 36/37  ÅLESUND
Öl auf Leinwand / Oil on canvas  70 x 90 cm  2010

SEITE 38/39  SCHNEE / SNOW
Öl auf Leinwand / Oil on canvas  55 x 70 cm  2008

LE SOLEIL LEVANT

Öl auf Leinwand /
Oil on canvas
200 x 100 cm
1997

SPIEGELUNG /
REFLECTION

Öl auf Leinwand /
Oil on canvas
200 x 100 cm  2006

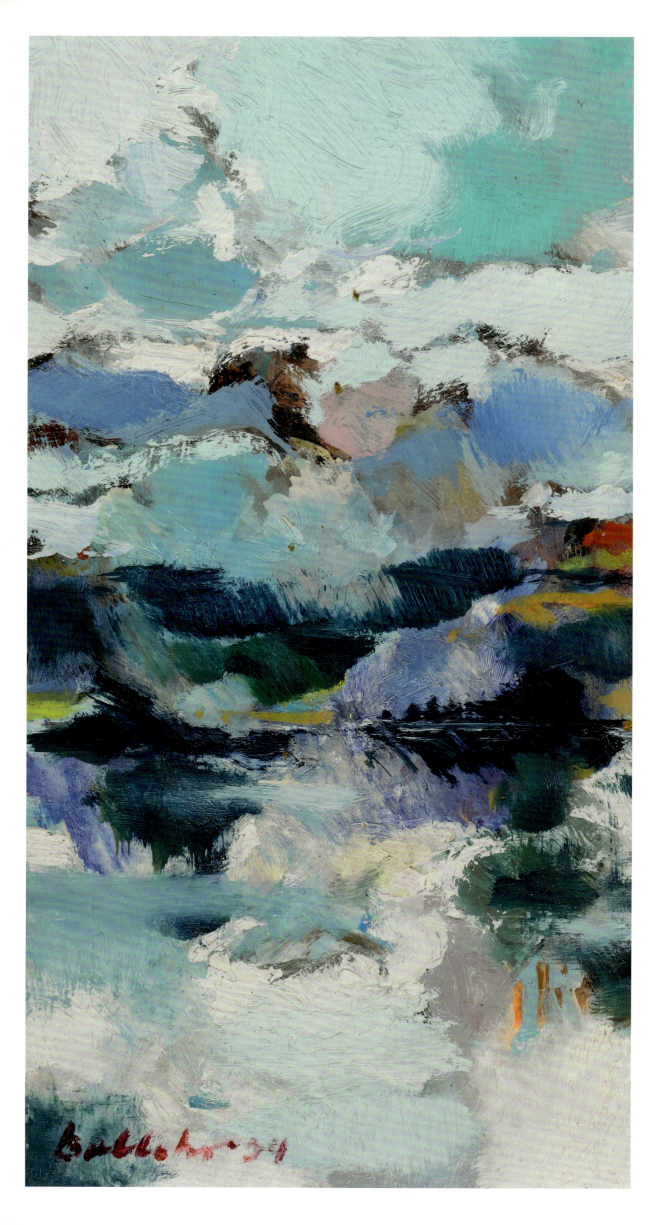

URI
Öl auf Holz /
Oil on wood
31 x 16 cm
1994

DURCHBRUCH
DES LICHTS /
LIGHT BREAKS
THROUGH

Öl auf Leinwand /
Oil on canvas
200 x 100 cm  1998

FELDER / FIELDS
Öl auf Leinwand / Oil on canvas  200 x 100 cm  2006

ABSCHIED DES LICHTS / LIGHT WANES
Öl auf Leinwand / Oil on canvas  200 x 100 cm  1980

DIE SCHÖPFUNG / THE CREATION
Acryl u. Öl auf Karton / Acrylic and oil on board
1500 x 500 cm  2007

Prospekt für das Oratorium „Die Schöpfung" von Haydn
Herz-Jesu-Kirche Stuttgart 2007

Prospectus for the oratorio "The Creation" by Haydn,
Heart-of-Jesus Church in Stuttgart

Hier ausgestellt im Hl. Kreuz Münster Schwäbisch Gmünd
bei der „Gmünder Art" 2008 mit einer Multi-Media-Show.

Exhibited here in the Holy Cross Minster in Schwäbisch Gmünd
at the "Gmünder Art" 2008 as part of a multi-media show.

Foto/Photo: Walter Laible

## NUDE AND FIGURE

When painting or drawing a nude, I always attempt
to capture the varied play of loading and supporting
forces on the human body. Standing, walking, sitting
or reclining become a multi-faceted "balancing act"
in contrapposto, during which any movement of
even the smallest part affects the whole form.
I am especially fascinated by the way in which shape
is given to the body in space by transverse bars of light.
Ideally, a few lines are enough for the nude to come alive.

Ballehr

## AKT UND FIGUR

Beim Akt versuche ich, das variationsreiche Spiel
stützender und lastender Kräfte am menschlichen Körper
zu gestalten.
Das Stehen, Gehen, Sitzen und Liegen stellt sich im
Kontrapost als vielgestaltige „Ballance-Aktion" dar.
Dabei laufen die Bewegungen in einem harmonischen
Rhythmus ab, bei dem jede Regung eines kleinsten Teils
auf die gesamte Gestalt rückwirkt.
Ganz besonders fasziniert mich, wie die durchlaufenden
Bahnen des Lichts den Körper im Raum formulieren.
Im Idealfall genügen wenige Linien und der Akt lebt.

                                                      Ballehr

RÜCKENTORSO MÄNNLICH / MALE TORSO, REAR VIEW
Kreide auf Papier / Chalk on paper  58 x 38 cm  2002

RÜCKENAKT WEIBLICH / FEMALE NUDE, REAR VIEW
Kohlestift auf Papier / Charcoal stick on paper  61 x 43 cm  1987

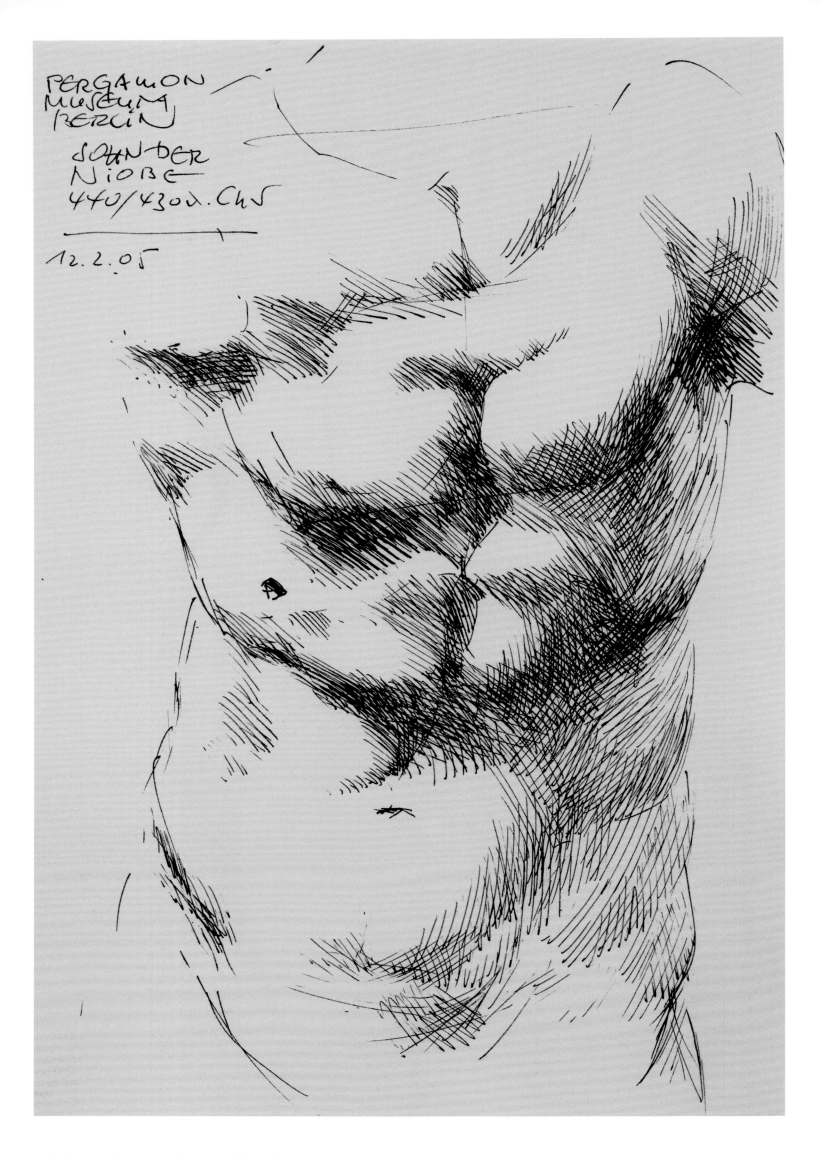

DER SOHN DER NIOBE / SON OF NIOBE
Tusche auf Papier / Indian ink on paper  28 x 18 cm  2005

RÜCKENAKT MÄNNLICH / MALE NUDE, REAR VIEW
Kreide auf Papier / Chalk on paper  61 x 43 cm  2002

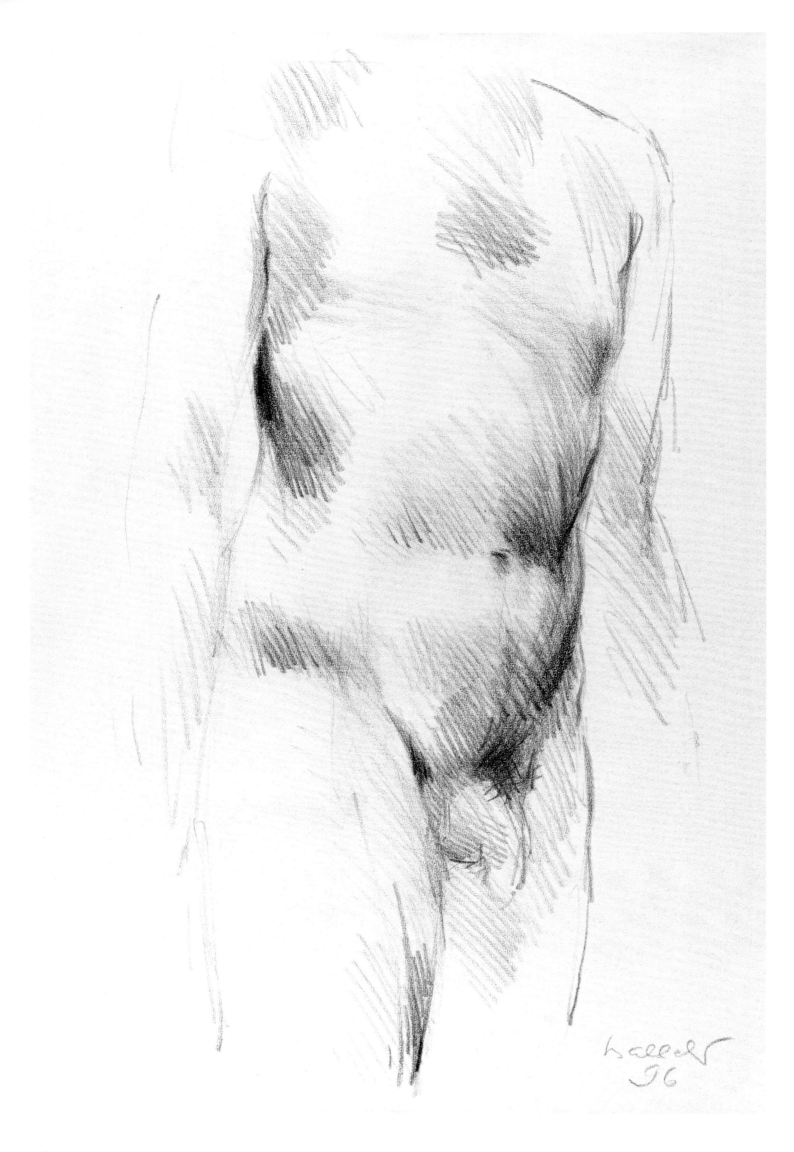

MÄNNLICHER TORSO / MALE TORSO
Kohle auf Papier / Charcoal on paper  62 x 48 cm  1996

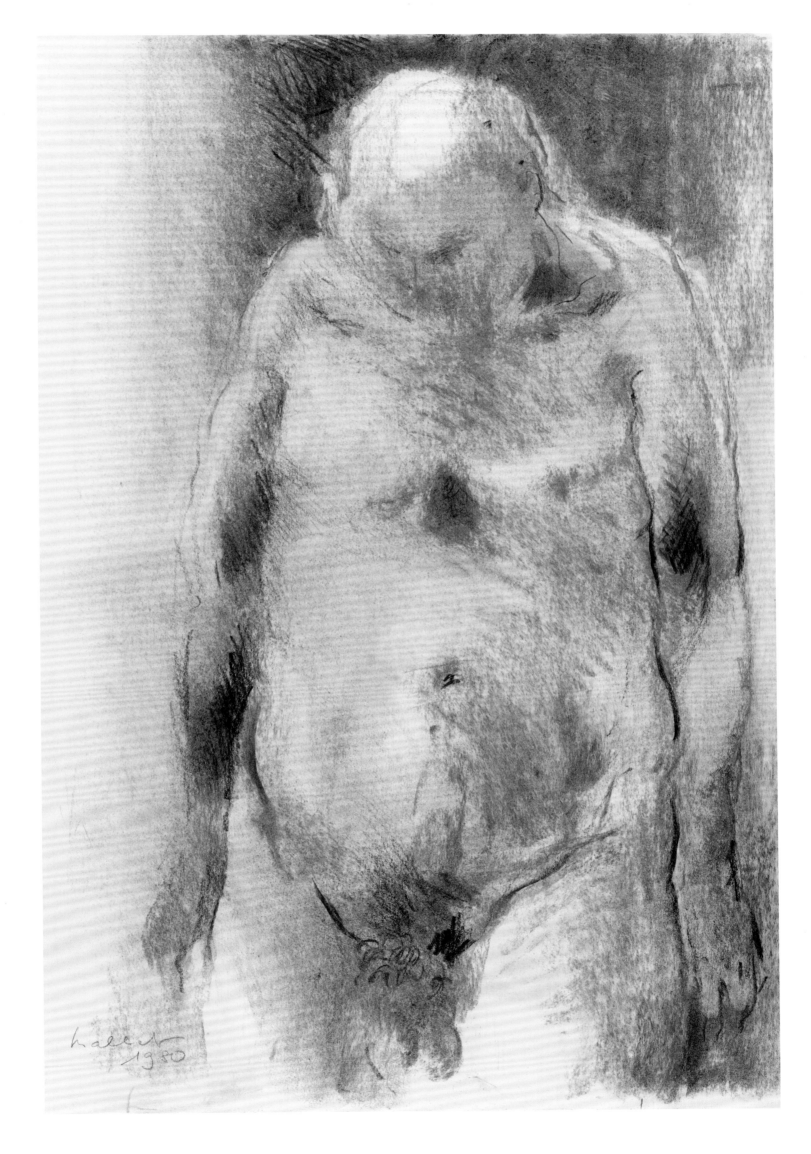

MÄNNLICHER TORSO / MALE TORSO
Kreide auf Papier / Chalk on paper  61 x 63 cm  1980

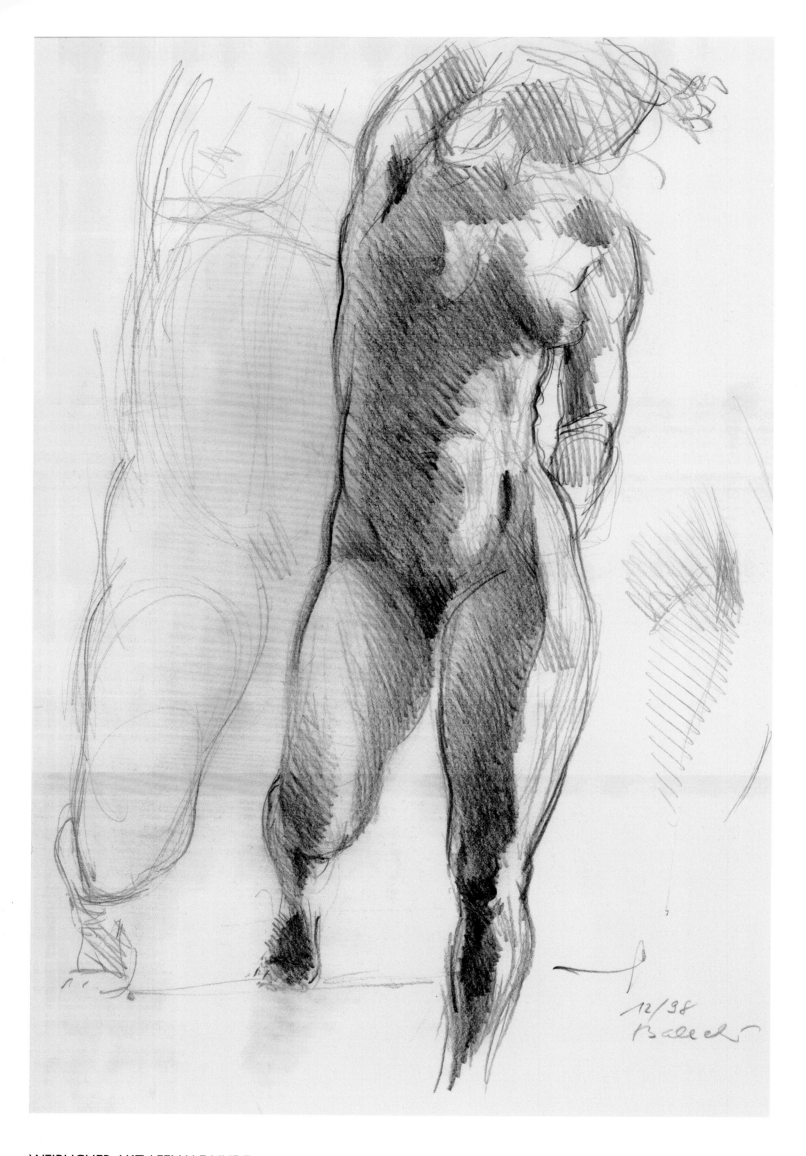

WEIBLICHER AKT / FEMALE NUDE
Kreide auf Papier / Chalk on paper  62 x 48 cm  1998

WEIBLICHER AKT / FEMALE NUDE
Kreide auf Papier / Chalk on paper  100 x 70 cm  1995

AKTE IN BEWEGUNG / MOVING NUDES
Kreide auf Papier / Chalk on paper  42 x 59,5 cm  1998

THIELLE
Kreide auf Papier / Chalk on paper  30 x 40 cm  1995

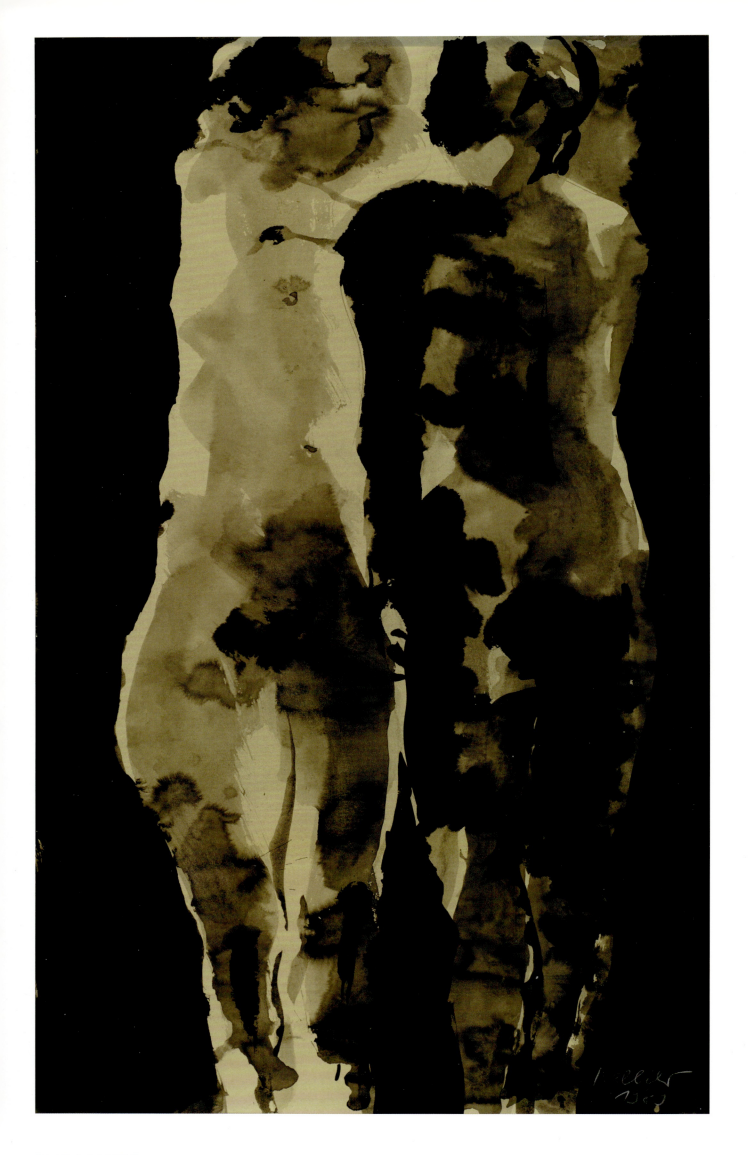

PAAR / COUPLE
Tusche auf Papier / Indian ink on paper  70 x 43 cm  1989

ZWEI AKTE / TWO NUDES
Öl auf Holz / Oil on wood  31 x 21 cm  1991

MALER UND MODELL /
ARTIST AND MODEL

Öl auf Leinwand /
Oil on canvas
100 x 50 cm 2001

WEIBLICHER AKT / FEMALE NUDE
Öl auf Holz / Oil on wood  50 x 35 cm  1990

PAAR / COUPLE
Öl auf Holz / Oil on wood  35,5 x 20 cm  2004

LIEBESPAAR UND TOD / TWO LOVERS AND DEATH
Öl auf Leinwand / Oil on canvas  130 x 100 cm  2001

MALER UND MODELL / ARTIST AND MODEL
Öl auf Holz / Oil on wood  50 x 35 cm  1986

MALER UND MODELL / ARTIST AND MODEL
Öl auf Holz / Oil on wood  50 x 35 cm  1994

MALER UND MODELL / ARTIST AND MODEL
Öl auf Leinwand / Oil on canvas  49 x 35 cm  1980

ZWEI FIGUREN / TWO FIGURES
Öl auf Holz / Oil on wood  50 x 35 cm  1980

MALER UND MODELL / ARTIST AND MODEL
Öl auf Holz / Oil on wood  70 x 49 cm  1986

MALER UND MODELL / ARTIST AND MODEL
Öl auf Holz / Oil on wood  50 x 35 cm  1986

IST'S MÖGLICH? / IS IT POSSIBLE?
Mischtechnik und Collage auf Papier / Mixed technique/collage on paper  42 x 64 cm  1991

SHOW
Mischtechnik und Collage / Mixed technique/collage  42 x 69 cm  1991

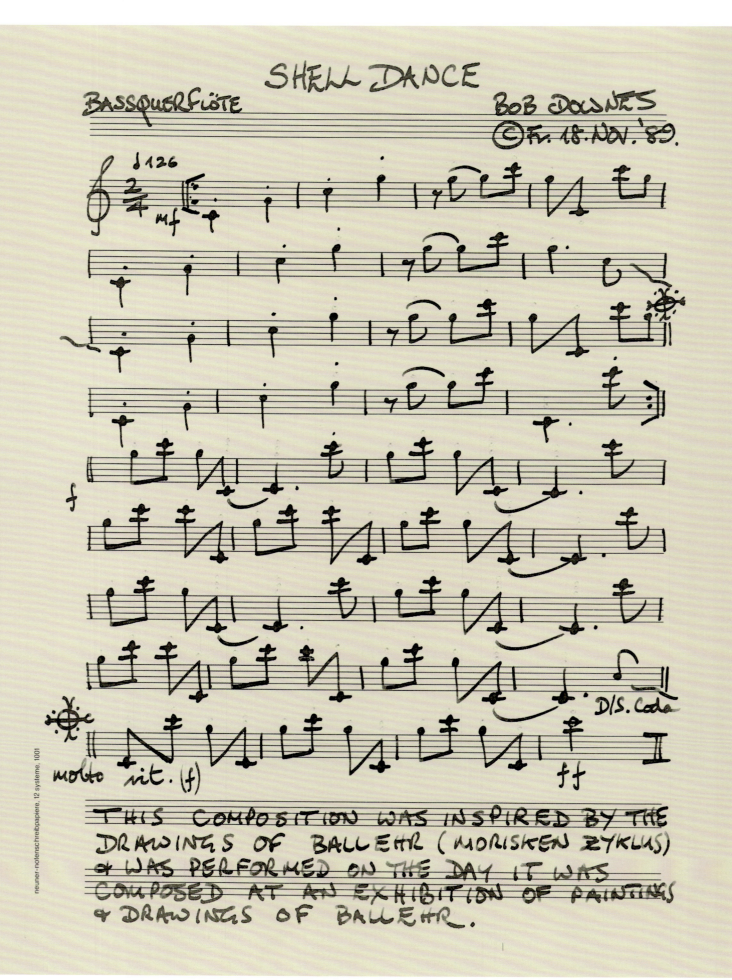

SHELLDANCE

Komposition von Bob Downes für Morisken-Zyklus 1989

SHELLDANCE

Kohle und Kreide auf Papier / Charcoal and chalk on paper  48 x 62 cm  1989

JAZZTANZ / JAZZ DANCE
Kreide auf Papier / Chalk on paper  35 x 24 cm  1990

JAZZTANZ / JAZZ DANCE
Kreide auf Papier / Chalk on paper  35 x 24 cm  1990

**TANZENDES PAAR / DANCING COUPLE**
Tusche auf Papier / Indian ink on paper  53,5 x 37,5 cm  1989

TANZENDES PAAR / DANCING COUPLE
Tusche und Kreide auf Papier / Indian ink and chalk on paper  61 × 36 cm  1989

ÄGYPTISCHE TÄNZERIN / EGYPTIAN DANCER
Öl auf Leinwand / Oil on canvas   100 x 50 cm   2008

THEATERVORHANG / THEATRE CURTAIN
Mischtechnik auf Papier / Mixed technique on paper  61 x 46 cm  1989

STRUMPFBAND / GARTER
Öl auf Holz / Oil on wood  25 x 8,5 cm  1994

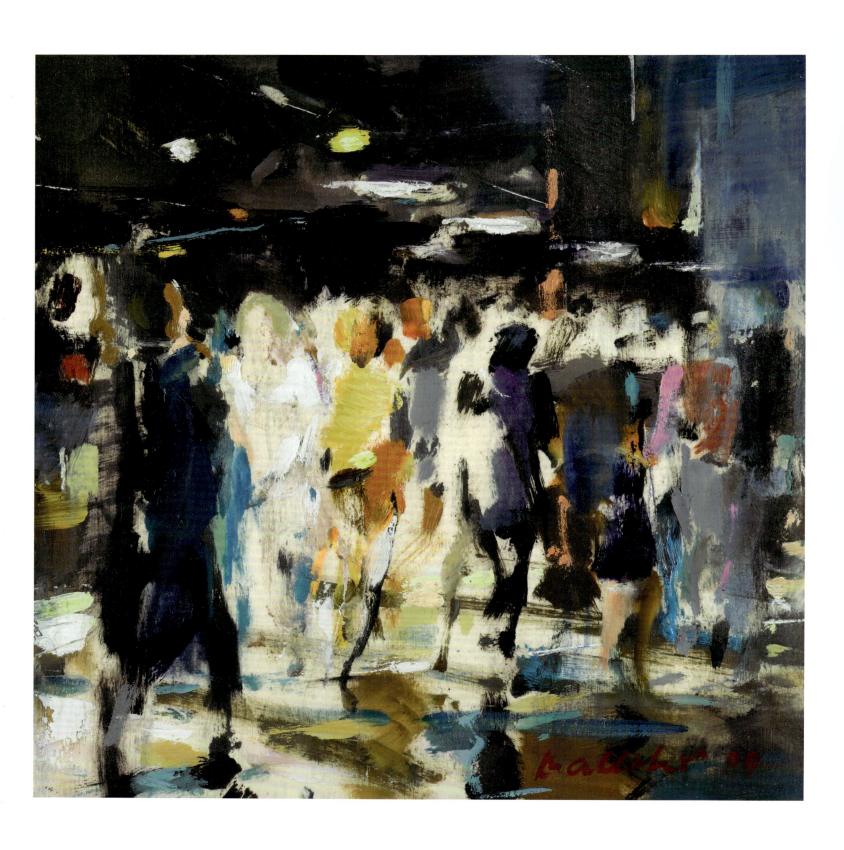

GROSSSTADT-IMPRESSION / TOWN IMPRESSIONS
Öl auf Holz / Oil on wood 42 x 42 cm 2009

GROSSSTADT-IMPRESSION / TOWN IMPRESSIONS
Öl auf Holz / Oil on wood  42 x 42 cm  2009

GROSSSTADT-IMPRESSION / TOWN IMPRESSIONS
Öl auf Holz / Oil on wood 42 x 42 cm 2009

IM REGEN / IN THE RAIN
Öl auf Holz / Oil on wood 24 x 18 cm 2001

ECCE HOMO

Among the motifs of my work there is a subject whose content goes beyond the mere formation of light and shade, beyond the compression and dissolution of bodies in light.

In the early 80s my paintings started to portray ominous figures, pursuing or threatening, and I soon realised that this particular motif had its roots not in past history but in urgently contemporary events.
The paintings were a subconscious reaction to the existence of the Pershing and SS20 rockets which were then provoking protest marches and blockades in Mutlangen. I called them "Ecce Homo paintings", although by this I meant not only the Passion of Christ, but man as such, persecuted, tortured and humiliated by other men, worldwide and in all ages.
Homo homini lupus.

Ballehr

## ECCE HOMO

Bei meinen Bildthemen gibt es ein Sujet, das inhaltlich hinausgeht über die reine Licht- und Schattengestaltung, über die Verdichtung und Auflösung der Körper im Licht.

In den frühen 80er Jahren entstanden düstere Figurenbilder der Verfolgung und Bedrohung, bei denen mir bald klar wurde, dass die Thematik nicht historischen, sondern höchst aktuellen Ursprungs war.
Die Bilder stellten eine unterschwellige Reaktion auf die Existenz der Pershing- und SS/20-Raketen dar, die damals in Mutlangen zu Protestmärschen und Blockaden führte.
Ich nannte sie „Ecce-Homo-Bilder", obgleich ich dabei nicht nur Christi Passion meinte, sondern den vom Menschen verfolgten, gequälten, gedemütigten Menschen an sich, weltweit und überzeitlich.
Homo homini lupus.

Ballehr

OHNMACHT / POWERLESS
Ölkreide auf Papier / Oil chalk on paper  70 x 50 cm  1984

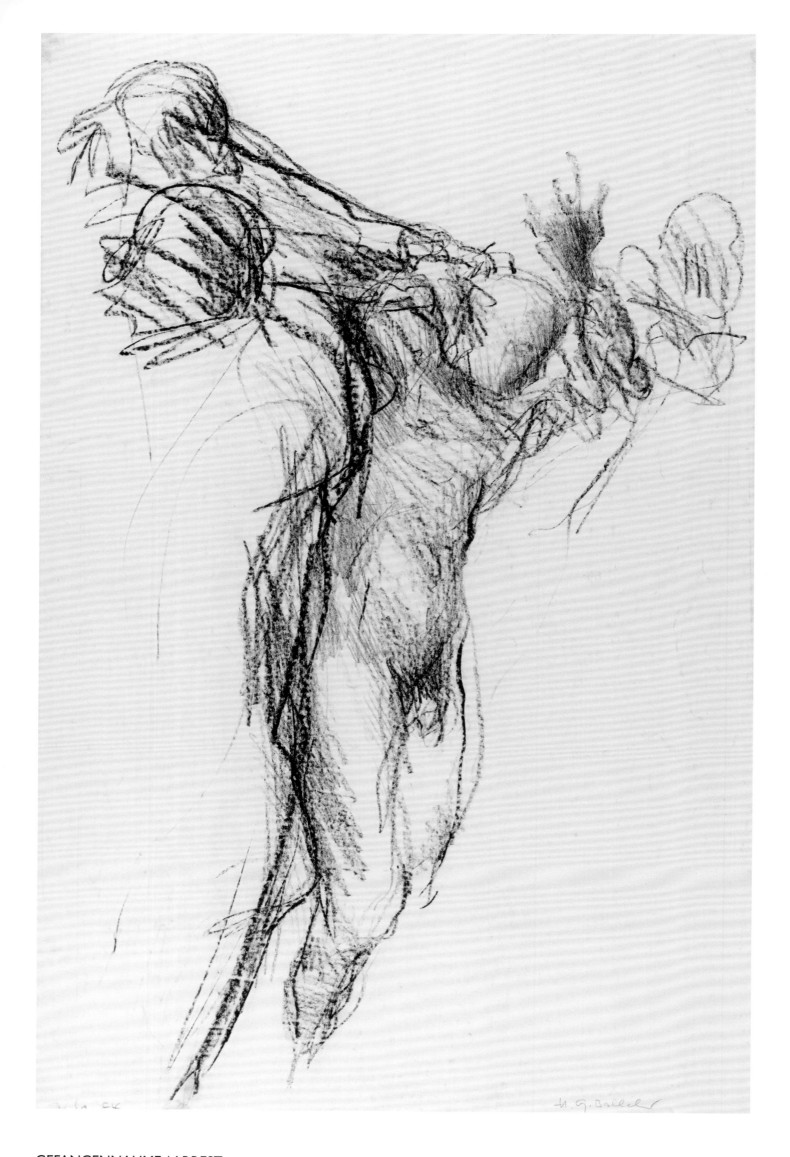

GEFANGENNAHME / ARREST
Ölkreide auf Papier / Oil chalk on paper  84 x 53 cm  1984

GEFANGENNAHME / ARREST
Ölkreide und Japanaqua auf Papier / Oil chalk and Japan aqua on paper  61 x 43 cm  2002

GEFANGENNAHME / ARREST
Wachskreide auf Papier / Wax chalk on paper  61 x 43 cm  1992

GEFANGENNAHME / ARREST
Kreide, Tusche, Sepia auf Papier / Chalk, Indian ink, sepia on paper  75 x 64 cm  1991

DES HAHNEN SCHREI / THE CROWING OF THE COCK
Ölkreide auf Papier / Charcoal on paper  75 x 50 cm  1988

GEFANGENNAHME / ARREST
Ölkreide auf Papier (Mischtechnik) / Oilchalk on paper (Mixed technique)  70 x 50 cm  1988

GEFANGENNAHME / ARREST
Michtechnik auf Papier / Mixed technique on paper  84 x 53 cm  1984

STIFTEST FRIEDEN TOD / YOU BRING PEACE DEATH
Ölkreide auf Papier / Oilchalk on paper  61 x 43 cm  1992

SIMPLICIUS
Monotypie / Monotype 43 x 61 cm 1980

VERSCHWÖRUNG / PLOT
Kohle und Acryl auf Leinwand / Charcoal and acrylic on canvas  130 x 100 cm  1982

VERFOLGUNG / PERSECUTION
Kohle und Öllasur auf Leinwand / Charcoal and oil varnish on canvas  130 x 100 cm  1982

ANRUF / THE CALL
Kohle auf Papier/ Charcoal on paper 60 x 47 cm 1983

"ACH DU?" / "OH, IS IT YOU?"
Öl auf Holz / Oil on wood  50 x 40 cm  1983

SALOME
Acryl, Ölkreide und Öl auf Leinwand / Acrylic, oilchalk and oil on canvas  130 x 100 cm  1986

SALOME
Acryl und Öl auf Leinwand / Acrylic and oil on canvas  130 x 100 cm  1986

RITTER, TOD UND TEUFEL / KNIGHT, DEATH AND DEVIL
Öl auf Leinwand / Oil on canvas  130 x 100 cm  1983

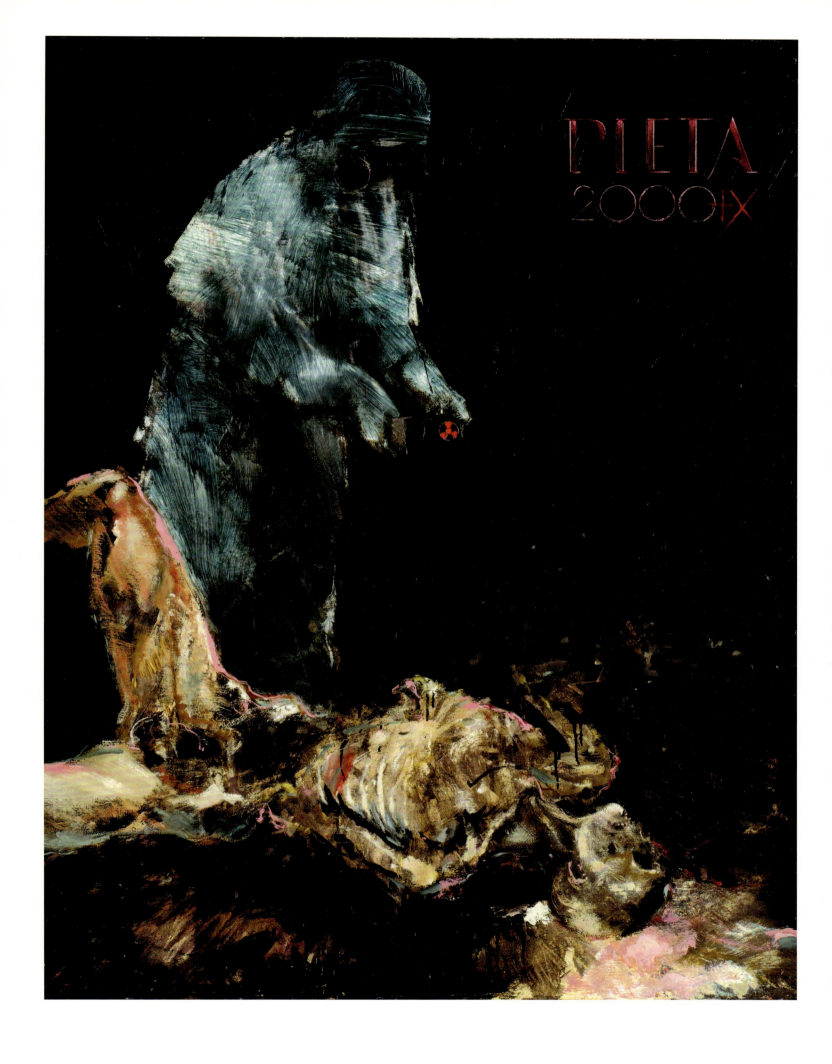

PIETA 2000+X
Öl und Acryl auf Leinwand / Oil and acrylic on canvas 143 x 120 cm  1991

INFERNO
Acryl und Öl auf Leinwand / Acrylic and oil on canvas   130 x 100 cm   1986

GEISSELUNG / SCOURGING
Acryl und Öl auf Leinwand / Acrylic and oil on canvas   200 x 100 cm   1989-1990

GEBUNDENER / MAN BOUND
Acryl auf Holz / Acrylic on wood   200 x 50 cm   1992

TOTENBRETT / THE BIER
Acryl auf Holz / Acrylic on wood   180 x 50 cm   1996

TOTENBRETT / THE BIER
Acryl auf Holz / Acrylic on wood   180 x 50 cm   1996

GEWALT / VIOLENCE
Ölkreide und Öl auf Leinwand / Oil chalk and oil on canvas  200 x 100 cm  1990

AUSGELIEFERT / HANDED OVER
Öl auf Leinwand / Oil on canvas  200 x 100 cm  1982

HOMO
Acryl auf Leinwand
Acrylic on canvas
200 x 100 cm  1982

HOMO
Öl auf Leinwand
Oil on canvas
200 x 100 cm  1984

PIETA RONDANINI
Öl auf Leinwand / Oil on canvas  200 x 100 cm  1982

Erster Preis beim Wettbewerb „Zeit-Zeichen", Stuttgart  1983
First prize in "Zeit-Zeichen" competition, Stuttgart 1983

KREUZABNAHME / DESCENT FROM THE CROSS
Öl auf Leinwand / Oil on canvas  200 x 100 cm  1990

AM PFAHL / THE WHIPPING POST
Öl auf Leinwand / Oil on canvas  200 x 100 cm  1983-1985

PIETA
Acryl, Kohle, Öl auf Leinwand / Acrylic, charcoal, oil on canvas   130 x 100 cm   1982

IM KÖNIGSMANTEL / CLOTHED IN PURPLE
Öl auf Leinwand / Oil on canvas  130 x 100 cm  1991

**Crucifixus**
Öl und Ölkreide auf Leinwand / Oil and oil chalk on canvas  200 x 100 cm  2008

CRUCIFIXUS
Öl auf Leinwand / Oil on canvas  200 x 100 cm  1984-1986

Ausstellung: ECCE HOMO Martinskirche Sindelfingen 1993
Exhibition: ECCE HOMO St Martin's Church, Sindelfingen 1993

AUSSTELLUNG ECCE HOMO /
EXHIBITION ECCE HOMO
in der Johanniskirche Schwäbisch Gmünd 1991
St John's Church Schwäbisch Gmünd 1991

MISERICORDIA
Öl und Acryl auf Leinwand / Oil and acrylic on canvas 130 x 100 cm 1982

SEITE 184/185:
HOMO
Öl auf Leinwand / Oil on canvas 200 x 100 cm 1984

PER ASPERA
Öl und Acryl auf Leinwand / Oil and acrylic on canvas 200 x 100 1990

AUSSTELLUNG ECCE HOMO /
EXHIBITION ECCE HOMO
Johanniskirche Schwäbisch Gmünd
St John's Church Schwäbisch Gmünd

DIE SIEBENTE SCHALE /
THE SEVENTH VIAL

Mischtechnik auf Karton /
Mixed technique on board
700 x 350 cm　　　1991

PORTRAIT

My sketchbooks are filled with portrait drawings.
Why?
Is there anything more interesting than to read in the human countenance?
The purpose of such portrait sketches was brought out by Andrei Monoky in Paris in 1962, when he said to me, "You have drawn my soul."

Ballehr

## PORTRAIT

Meine Skizzenbücher sind gefüllt mit Portraitzeichnungen.
Warum?
Gibt es etwas Interessanteres, als in menschlichen
Gesichtern zu lesen?
Den Sinn derartiger Protraitskizzen hat Andreï Monoky
1962 in Paris benannt, als er zu mir sagte:
„Du hast meine Seele gezeichnet."

                                                                        Ballehr

VIDI
Kreide auf Papier / Chalk on paper  29 x 21 cm  1986

ZORN / RAGE
Kreide auf Papier / Chalk on paper  29 x 21 cm  1986

SANDRA W.
Kreide auf Papier / Chalk on paper  63 x 48 cm  1979

SEPP B. ALS FAUN / SEPP B. AS A FAUN
Lithografie / Lithograph 41 x 31 cm 1986

LARA UND SERGEJ
Kohle auf Papier / Charcoal on paper  40 x 57,5 cm  1980

MORISKEN / MORESCOS
Kohle auf Papier / Charcoal on paper  50 x 60 cm  1989

LA BELLE
Tusche und Kreide auf Papier / Indian ink and chalk on paper  64,5 × 47,5 cm  1989

TINNY

links: Kohle auf Papier / left: Charcoal on paper   52 x 35 cm   1979

rechts: Öl auf Holz / right: Oil on wood   91 x 74 cm   1979

BÄRBELE
Öl auf Holz / Oil on wood  70 x 49 cm  1980

## STILL LIFE

"Still life: what a strange term! As if to deny that here wizardry is in the air: the magic of creation." (Benedikt Erenz, Fruits from Light: Willem Kalf's magic paintings, Zeitmagazin No. 30, 1993, P. 14).
I admire Kalf's small still life from 1653 in the Alte Pinakothek in Munich. However, I myself do not paint "still lifes".
I do not merely reproduce fruit and glasses, neither as symbols of wealth nor as symbols of vanity. I paint density and light! But light only becomes visible when there is an object for it to illuminate.
On canvas, light can only be represented by "light equation", using coloured shadows and strong contrasts between light and dark. This is the reason for the richly dim, but never black, darkness of my backgrounds, before which matter is compressed and again dissolves, floating in light and shade.
Being optically immaterial, glass is a particularly tempting subject: this colourless matter, with its unearthly transparency and with the infinitely varied play of highlights on its smooth, hard, crystalline surface. But the only way to paint glass is not to paint it! Light is everything!
"Light, nothing but light." (Erenz, ibid.)

Ballehr

## STILLLEBEN

„Stilleben, was für ein seltsames Wort!
Als sei hier nicht Magie im Spiel: Schöpfungszauber."
(Benedikt Erenz, Früchte aus Licht, Willem Kalfs
magische Bilder, Zeitmagazin 30, 1993 S.14)
Ich bewundere Kalfs kleines Stillleben von 1653 in der
Alten Pinakothek. Aber ich selbst male nicht „Stillleben".
Ich male keine Früchte und Gläser ab, weder als
Preziosen noch als Vanitas-Symbole.
Ich male Dichte und Licht! Licht aber wird nur sichtbar,
wenn es auf Körper trifft.
Auf der Leinwand ist Licht nur darstellbar in Form der
„Lichtgleichung", durch große Hell-Dunkel-Kontraste
und durch die Farbigkeit der Schatten. Daher die sonore,
doch niemals schwarze Dunkelheit der Gründe,
vor denen sich in einem Schwebezustand Gegenstände
verdichten und wieder auflösen in Licht und Schatten.
Mit seiner optischen Immaterialität ist Glas hier besonders
reizvoll; dieses farblose Material, mit seiner unirdischen
Durchsichtigkeit und mit dem vielfältigen Spiel der
Glanzlichter auf seiner glatten, harten, kristallinen Oberfläche.
Glas aber kann man nur malen, indem man es nicht malt!
Licht ist alles! „Licht, nichts als Licht" (Erenz, s.o.)

Ballehr

DICHTE UND LICHT / DENSITY AND LIGHT
Öl auf Leinwand / Oil on canvas  80 x 100 cm  2008

AMBIVALENZ / AMBIVALENCE
Öl auf Leinwand / Oil on canvas  80 x 100 cm  1991-1994

SPOT LIGHT
Öl auf Leinwand über Holz / Oil on canvas over wood 30 x 40,5 cm  1994

ALTER KLANG (KLEE) / OLD SOUND (KLEE)
Öl auf Holz / Oil on wood   30 x 40 cm   1999

FARBE IST EIN HAUCH / COLOUR IS BUT A BREATH
Öl auf Leinwand / Oil on canvas   100 x 80 cm   1991-1994

Farbe ist ein Hauch,
erblüht, zerrinnt.
Was bleibt von dieser Welt?
Weiter führt mein Weg
mich heute hin
durch das Dickicht
eines kurzen Lebens.
Ich befreie mich
von schalen Träumen.
Sättigung.
(Hisako Matsubara)


Colour is but a breath,
a flower that blooms and fades.
What in this world lasts?
But today, my path
leads me ever onward,
passing through the thicket
of my short life.
Its dull dreams
fall away.
I see.

*Farbe ist ein Hauch  
erfüllt zerrinnt.  
Was bleibt von dieser Welt?  
Weiter führt mein Weg  
mich heute hin,  
durch das Dickicht  
eines herben Lebens.  
Ich befreie mich im Schlaf  
Träumen  
Sinnigung*

GLANZLICHTER / HIGHLIGHTS
Öl auf Leinwand / Oil on canvas   100 x 80 cm   2008

STILLLEBEN MIT MESSINGKESSEL / STILL LIFE WITH BRASS BOWL
Öl auf Leinwand / Oil on canvas  100 x 80 cm  2008

STILLLEBEN MIT MESSINGKESSEL / STILL LIFE WITH BRASS BOWL
Öl auf Leinwand / Oil on canvas  100 x 80 cm  2008

LICHTGLEICHUNG / LIGHT EQUATION
Öl auf Leinwand / Oil on canvas  100 x 80 cm  1994-1997

CLAIRE
Öl auf Leinwand / Oil on canvas  30 x 40 cm  2006

FRÜHLICHT / EARLY LIGHT
Öl auf Holz / Oil on wood  35 x 50 cm  1998

EINE SCHALE VOLL LICHT / A BOWLFUL OF LIGHT
Öl auf Holz / Oil on wood  31 x 41 cm  1995

FÜR ALMUTH / FOR ALMUTH
Öl auf Holz / Oil on wood  50 x 35 cm  1996

LICHT, NICHT ALS LICHT / LIGHT, NOTHING BUT LIGHT (ERENZ)
Öl auf Leinwand / Oil on canvas  100 x 80 cm  2008

## VITA

Dr. Helmut Maximilian Gruber-Ballehr,
geboren 1939 in München.
Verheiratet, drei Kinder.
Frühe künstlerische Anregungen durch Professor
Ernst August v. Mandelsloh, Kunstakademie Wien.
Studium an der Kunstakademie Stuttgart, bei den Professoren
Peters, Schellenberger, Yelin und Dr. Fegers. Staatsexamen.
Studium der Kunstgeschichte an der Universität Tübingen,
bei den Professoren Dr. Bandmann, Dr. Scheja und
Dr. de Chapeau Rouge. Promotion.
Lehrtätigkeit an der PH Schwäbisch Gmünd und an Gymnasien.
Mehrere Jahre freischaffende Tätigkeit als Maler, Graphiker
und Kunsttheoretiker. Künstlername Ballehr.
Studienreisen in England, Frankreich, Italien, Spanien,
Griechenland und Japan.
Längere Arbeitsaufenthalte in Norwegen, Tadschikistan,
Ungarn und den USA.
Seit 1980 zahlreiche Einzel- und Gruppenausstellungen
im In- und Ausland.
Ateliers in Schwäbisch Gmünd und München.


## BIOGRAPHY

Dr Helmut Maximilian Gruber-Ballehr,
born in Munich in 1939.
Married; three children.
Early artistic talent stimulated and encouraged by Prof. Ernst
August v. Mandelsloh, Viennese Academy of Art.
Graduation from the Stuttgart Academy of Art under
Professors Peters, Schellenberger, Yelin and Dr Fegers.
D.Phil. in History of Art at the University of Tübingen,
under Professors Dr Bandmann, Dr Scheja and
Dr de Chapeau Rouge.
Lecturer at the Schwäbisch Gmünd Teacher Training College
and secondary school teacher.
Several years as independent painter, draughtsman and writer
on artistic theory. Artist's signature: Ballehr.
Study trips to England, France, Italy, Spain, Greece and Japan.
Extended working trips to Norway, Tajikistan, Hungary and USA.
From 1980 onwards, numerous one-man and group exhibitions
at home and abroad.
Studios in Schwäbisch-Gmünd and Munich.

AUSSTELLUNGEN / ) EXHIBITIONS

Gruppenausstellungen und Wettbewerbe mit dem BBK (VBKW), dem DKV Rottenburg, dem KV Gmünd und anderen Vereinigungen in München, Stuttgart, Köngen, Schw. Hall, Reichenau, Ellwangen, Osnabrück, Antibes, Szekesfehervar, Moskau, Dushanbe u.a.

Group exhibitions and competitions with the BBK (VBKW), the DKV Rottenburg, the KV Gmünd and other associations in Munich, Stuttgart, Köngen, Schw. Hall, Reichenau, Ellwangen, Osnabrück, Antibes, Szekesfehervar, Moscow, Dushanbe et al.

Einzelaustellungen / One-man exhibitions

1980 Städtisches Museum Schwäbisch Gmünd

1982 Kunstforum, Bad Cannstatt

1983 Galerie Johanning, Mannheim

1984 Städtische Galerie, Schwäbisch Gmünd

1987 Galerie Kunstforum, Schwäbisch Gmünd

1989 Galerie Videmus, Freiburg i.Br.

1990 Galerie Kanold u. Tallen, München / Munich

1991 Galerie Videmus, Freiburg i.Br.
    Johanniskirche, Schwäbisch Gmünd

1992 Lukaskirche, München / Munich

1993 Martinskirche, Sindelfingen

1995 St. Bernhard, Schwäbisch Gmünd

1996 Kloster Schöntal a.d. Jagst

1997 Galerie Schöne, Schwäbisch Gmünd
    Volksbank, Oberkochen

1998 Forum II, München / Munich

1999 Johanniskirche, Schwäbisch Gmünd

2000 Augustinuskirche, Schwäbisch Gmünd

2001 Kulturzentrum Bethlehem PA, USA

2002 Ostalbkreishaus, Aalen
    Bürgerhaus, Wasseralfingen

2003 Merkurbank, München / Munich
    Galerie Maier, Elchingen

2006 Städt. Galerie Szekesfehervar, Ungarn / Hungary

2007 Bruder-Klaus-Kirche und Herz-Jesu-Kirche, Stuttgart

2008 Rathausgalerie und Marienkirche, Aalen

2010 Galerie Kanold u. Tallen, München / Munich

2012 geplant: Peter- und Paulskirche, Esslingen

DANK

Sehr herzlich danke ich
meiner lieben Frau Almuth und unseren Freunden Pfarrer Dieter Müller
und Dr. Martin Diem für ihre Anregungen,
Frau Dr. Gabriele Holthuis, für das Lektorat und die Herausgabe,
meinem Schwiegersohn Bernhard Gruber-Ballehr für die Erstellung der Abbildungen,
Herrn Christopher Sloan für die Übersetzung der Texte ins Englische,
Frau Johanna Dolderer für ihre Arbeit am Layout, Frau Brigitte Nagel
und Herrn Jörg Schumacher für die Organisation,
sowie den folgenden Sponsoren für ihre großzügigen Spenden zu
dieser Monographie.


ACKNOWLEDGEMENT

My especial thanks to
my dear wife Almuth and to our friends Reverend Dieter Müller and
Dr Martin Diem for their suggestions,
Dr Gabriele Holthuis for proofreading and editing,
my son-in-law Bernhard Gruber-Ballehr for the photography,
Mr Christopher Sloan for the translation of the texts into English,
Mrs Johanna Dolderer for the layout, Mrs Brigitte Nagel and
Mr Jörg Schumacher for the organisation
and the following sponsors for the generous support of this monograph.

Eduard Dietenberger
Stiftung

IMPRESSUM

Herausgeber
Dr. Gabriele Holthuis
Dr. Helmut Maximilian Gruber-Ballehr
www.ballehr.com

Gesamtherstellung
Einhorn-Verlag+Druck GmbH
Sebaldplatz 1, Telefon 07171/92780-0
D-73525 Schwäbisch Gmünd

Druck
Fischer Druck, Schwäbisch Gmünd-Herlikofen

Alle Rechte, insbesondere das Recht der Vervielfältigung, Verbreitung und Übersetzung vorbehalten. Kein Teil des Werks darf in irgendeiner Form ohne schriftliche Genehmigung reproduziert oder unter Verwendung elektronischer Systeme verarbeitet, vervielfältigt oder verbreitet werden.

ISBN 978-3-936373-68-4

1. Auflage November 2011
Printed in Germany

© 2011
Dr. Helmut Maximilian Gruber-Ballehr